How to Make
Any Occasion Special

Creative Ideas for Everyday Living

by
Judie Byrd

HOW TO MAKE ANY OCCASION SPECIAL: Creative Ideas for Everyday Living
Copyright © 1994 by Judy Byrd

All Scripture quotations used in this book are from the New International Version of the Bible (NIV),
copyright © 1978 by the New York International Bible Society. Used by permission.

Library of Congress Cataloging-in-Publication Data

Byrd, Judie.
      How to make any occasion special / Judie Byrd.
         p.   cm.—(Quick-me-ups)
        ISBN 0-8499-3585-7
       1. Entertaining—Miscellanea.   I. Title.   II. Title: How to make any occasion special.
TX731.B97   1994
642'.4—dc20   94–5580
                                                       CIP

Printed in the United States of America.

Foreword

Countless women, including myself, have attended Judie Byrd's food and entertaining seminars. We've learned fabulous food ideas, surprisingly simple entertaining tips, and delightful ways to turn special occasions into treasured memories. Judie's audiences come away inspired and encouraged that it doesn't take a lot of money to entertain with flair. We don't need to study cooking in Europe (although Judie has) to serve a delicious, elegant meal. We don't have to schedule large blocks of time to create an event that will be a special memory for our families and friends. And it's the simple personal touches that can turn ordinary moments into extraordinary memories.

If you've never been to one of Judie's seminars, or if you've been to many of them, let me just say that you are in for a treat with this book. Judie not only teaches and demonstrates hundreds of creative ideas on stage and in print, but actually lives out her ideas daily with her own family and friends.

Throughout our eighteen-year friendship, I've never ceased being amazed. I've witnessed Judie make hundreds of occasions special—birthdays, dinner parties, weddings, brunches, showers, Thanksgiving and other holiday feasts, office parties, political fundraising events, award ceremonies, and midnight breakfasts.

And it's not only occasions. Judie regularly turns ordinary days into memorable moments as well. I've seen her bake twelve hundred cookies to hand out to students on a university campus when her son ran for student body president. She's served a surprise picnic lunch to maintenance men working at her house. She's baked wedding cakes and turned her backyard into an outdoor chapel for a friend's wedding.

How to Make Any Occasion Special *is a book for every woman who wants her home to be a place where family members and friends feel loved and welcome and regularly enjoy special occasions together. It's a book for women who understand that memories are being made—whether we realize it or not—every day of our families' existence. (There's a lot we can do to make these memories good ones.) And it's a book for women who don't have much extra time, money, or energy to make this happen. Judie Byrd has come to the rescue.*

Kathy Peel
Spring, 1994

Create whimsical salad bowls from bell peppers. Cut one-half inch off the top of each pepper and remove seeds. Fill with vegetable or pasta salads.

Create a fun picnic memory for kids by serving cupcakes decorated with plastic ants.

Make inexpensive taper candles look like fancy, expensive candles by painting designs on them with non-toxic, non-flammable T-shirt paints.

Serve scented sugar to add pizazz to ordinary coffee. Store one vanilla bean in a pint jar of sugar for a few days.

Create birthday cone cakes. Fill flat-bottomed ice cream cones one-third full with cake batter. Bake according to instructions for cupcakes. When cool, top with a scoop of ice cream and a birthday candle.

Freeze mint leaves, strawberry slices, or kiwi slices in ice cubes to dress up a glass of ordinary iced tea.

"Research tells us that fourteen out of any ten individuals like chocolate." —Sandra Boynton

Dip coffee beans in melted chocolate and place on waxed paper to dry. Serve with coffee for an elegant treat.

Make elegant poached pears by simmering peeled pears in cranberry juice until tender.

Use a star-shaped cookie cutter to cut bread for lunchbox sandwiches the day your child is in a school play. Include a note that says, "You're always a star to me!"

Put pink light bulbs in lamps and light fixtures to create a warm ambiance in a room.

Use terra-cotta pot saucers as dinner plates when serving Mexican food.

For a gourmet dessert, fill a chocolate layer cake with raspberry jam and frost it with whipped cream.

Have a western party. Make a centerpiece by arranging tall, dried flowers in a cowboy boot. Carry out the theme with a tablecloth made from ordinary burlap. Use raffia to tie up cutlery in bandanna napkins and have metal pie pans for plates. Serve nachos, bean dip, or other western-style food in cast-iron frying pans. Tie a bandanna around the pan handles to brighten them up.

Tie up napkins with satin ribbon or gold cording to give them a special look. Tuck in a piece of seasonal greenery or small flower.

Create a glamorous atmosphere on a party table by tying up a small piece of dry ice in cheesecloth and putting it into a bowl of punch. (There will be a lot of smoke, but the punch won't be affected.)

Host a "Poorhouse Party" for friends on April 15th. For invitations, make photocopies of income-tax return forms and write party details with a red marker.

Use cinnamon sticks as stirrers for coffee or hot cocoa.

Use non-poisonous fresh flowers to turn an ordinary cake into a fabulous dessert. Fill small plastic water picks (available at florists) halfway with water and insert flowers. Push them into the top of a frosted cake.

Make interesting ice-cream shapes by packing ice cream into gelatin molds. Freeze hard, then unmold on a plate.

Serve your own "Cookie Dough Ice Cream." Make a batch of cookie dough, roll it into little balls and freeze until firm. Stir frozen dough balls into softened ice cream, then refreeze.

If you only have time to either clean your house or bake cookies to celebrate your child making a good grade on a test, go for the cookies.

"We have left undone those things which we ought to have done; and we have done those things which we ought not to have done."

—The Book of Common Prayer

Fix a fun fall lunch. Carve out miniature pumpkins and fill them with chicken, tuna, or pasta salad.

For a last-minute celebration, hang curly ribbon from the chandelier over your dining table. Tie small balloons onto the ribbons at different levels.

Keep ice-cream snowballs handy for dessert. Scoop large ice-cream balls and quickly roll each one in coconut. Place them on a tray lined with waxed paper, then freeze. To serve, spoon chocolate sauce in the bottom of individual dishes and set a snowball on top.

For a child's slumber party, make a giant sugar cookie on a round pizza pan. Let children decorate it with icing, candies, and colored sprinkles.

Don't wait for Christmas to put swags of green garland on your staircase. Dress up your banister for a spring or summer occasion with seasonal flowers and ivy interspersed in a grapevine garland.

Create a pretty buffet table by pinning trails and loops of ivy and ribbon around the edge of the tablecloth.

"Let us endeavor so to live that when we come to die even the undertaker will be sorry."

—Mark Twain

Make it a priority to regularly do simple things that will turn minutes into memorable moments. You'll enjoy life more and so will those around you.

Store ironed tablecloths on hangers so they are ready to use.

Keep a stash of little gifts to make a big deal out of a child making progress in a particular area—studying harder, helping without being asked, treating others kindly.

Compose a song, poem, or story about a special day. Give it to someone you love.

"*A good host puts the first stain on the tablecloth.*"
—Anonymous

Aim to make your home fun, warm, and inviting, instead of impressive and intimidating.

On St. Patrick's Day, use a cookie cutter to cut sandwich bread into shamrocks. Fill with green-tinted cream cheese.

Pull off impromptu picnics with ease by keeping a picnic basket stocked with plastic cutlery, paper plates, cups, and napkins.

Sew lace on the edges of plain bathroom towels to give them a fancy look for guests.

Give a flag cake to a veteran on a patriotic holiday. Bake a nine-by-thirteen-inch cake and frost it with white icing. Line up red jelly beans for the stripes, and place blue jelly beans in the corner for stars.

"Life, within doors, has few pleasanter prospects than a neatly arranged and well-provisioned breakfast table."
　　　　　　　　　　　　　　　—Nathaniel Hawthorne
Give your family a great send-off in the morning by adding a little butter and cinnamon to maple syrup and serving it warm with pancakes.

Use little tagged gifts instead of place cards at a dinner party.

Turn an ordinary weekend day into a fun memory with friends. Split the cost of several baskets of fruit in season —apples, blueberries, strawberries. Schedule a day to get together and enjoy baking, canning, or freezing for future use.

Start a party-idea file. Clip magazine pictures of decorations, table settings, and centerpieces to give you instant inspiration.

The secret to encouraging good conversation at a dinner party is to have tables that seat six to eight. Four people may run out of conversation topics, and a table for ten may intimidate some.

"Do not wait for extraordinary circumstances to do good actions; try to use ordinary situations."

—Jean Paul Richter

Send someone you care about a greeting card with a warm message for no other reason than to say that you care.

Float primroses or pansies in a bowl of water for a charming table centerpiece.

When writing the guestlist for a party, keep in mind your friends' interests and try to invite others they will enjoy.

Three weeks before a winter party, plant paper-white narcissus bulbs. You'll have elegant, growing flowers.

Videotape your child's music recital or class play for long-distance grandparents. Add a special we-miss-you message at the end.

Let your kids be servers, door openers, or coat checkers at a party. Use paint pens to decorate T-shirts to look like tuxedos for them to wear. Buy inexpensive plastic top hats at a costume or toy store.

Add flair to desserts. Put candles in clip-on candle-holders (the kind usually used on Christmas trees) and attach them around the edge of a tray from which you serve a fancy dessert.

If school's out because of snow, have a neighborhood snowman contest. See who can create the biggest, fanciest, and most unique snowman. Take photos, award small prizes, and serve hot cocoa to all.

"The secret of success in life is for a man to be ready for his opportunity when it comes."

—Benjamin Disraeli

Be party-ready. Keep a drawer stocked with paper goods, balloons, candles, confetti, and streamers. Keep beverages, canned nuts, and other appetizers on hand.

Pick up old silver spoons at flea markets and have a silversmith bend the ends into napkin rings.

Allow two tall candles for each candlestick during a party. Candles will burn longer when stored in the refrigerator.

Use a felt-tip calligraphy pen to address party invitations. Add stickers to the invitation or the envelope for pizazz.

Bring home postcards when you visit a museum. Use them for interesting invitations to a dinner party.

Collect old Mirro™ gelatin molds to make interesting ice molds to float in a punch bowl.

To instantly dress up a table, scatter small sprays of seasonal greenery among the dishes.

Serve Cake on a Cloud for a fancy dessert. Buy bags of cotton candy. Place a "cloud" of the candy on each plate. Place a slice of cake on top of the cloud, and top it with a dollop of ice cream.

Pleasant background music enhances the atmosphere of any occasion. Ask a local music store to help you find selections by Mozart, Beethovan, or Vivaldi for a dinner party. Country-and-western music adds flair to a casual cookout.

"He who waits to do a great deal at once will never do anything." —Charles Simmons

Don't think you have to go to elaborate extremes. Many times it's small, simple touches that make something ordinary extraordinary.

For a fun invitation, write party details on a balloon and attach a note instructing the recipient to blow it up.

Get a baby picture of each of your party guests (Make copies so you can return the original.) Mount them all on a piece of poster board. Give a prize to the person who identifies the most.

Place smooth river rocks, sea shells, or colored marbles in the bottom of clear vases to anchor flowers.

Keep various sizes and colors of paper doilies on hand. Use them to line baskets, to dress up a plate of cookies, as drink coasters, or for place mats.

Encourage your teenagers to invite their friends over after a ball game or party for a midnight breakfast. Serve breakfast burritos. Fill bowls with cooked sausage, shredded cheese, chopped green chilies, tomatoes, green peppers, and salsa. Provide warm tortillas and let them make their own burritos.

When you have small children at an event, create a table just for them. Cover the table with craft paper. Use markers to draw pretend place mats at each seat. Put a cup of markers on the table for the children to decorate their place mats.

"We find in life exactly
what we put into it."
—Ralph Waldo Emerson

The little extras we do to make
occasions memorable add
richness to life.

Start a tradition of Sunday nights being "Family Chef Night." Let family members take turns preparing their favorite foods. Buy a chef's hat and apron for the chef of the night to wear.

Straw beach mats make great table coverings for picnics and informal buffets. To clean, simply spray with a hose and let dry.

Set a goal to plan fun occasions with family and friends regularly.

Keep a large hurricane lamp on hand to make a decoration for any occasion. Fill it with seasonal items such as small pumpkins, oranges and walnuts, apples, glass Christmas balls, or dyed eggs. Tie a raffia or plaid bow around the top and surround the hurricane with greenery.

Have a child's drawing made into your Christmas card at a local printer.

Design a festive walkway to your front door by tying balloons onto stakes along the path.

Create gourmet peanut-butter sandwiches by making your own peanut butter. Put two cups of roasted, shelled peanuts and two teaspoons of vegetable oil into a food processor and grind until smooth. Add salt to taste.

Plan a "This Is Your Life" celebration on a loved one's birthday. Look at old photos and tell stories from the past. Tell the honoree how much his life means to you.

For a quick and festive centerpiece, carve out the middle of several apples to use as votive candleholders. Arrange them on a bed of magnolia leaves.

String small white Christmas lights on large house plants. Turn off the overhead lights for a beautiful atmosphere any time of the year.

You don't need a big dining room or fancy furniture to host a wonderful party. Use stereo speakers, stools, bookcases, the top of a piano, or a sturdy ironing board covered with a pretty quilt to hold hors d'oeuvres and buffet foods.

Line the inside of a
cowboy hat with a red bandanna.
Fill it with nuts or popcorn.

At a dinner party, serve dessert in a different room to change conversation groups.

"The wise man will make more opportunities than he finds." —Francis Bacon

Look for everyday happenings to celebrate—a young child losing her first tooth, a high-school senior getting accepted into college, or Dad closing a big deal.

Fill a plain glass pitcher to the brim with ice cubes, lemon and orange slices, and water.

Make a snazzy candleholder by trimming a candle-size hole from the middle of an artichoke. Spray it with gold spray paint, let it dry, then insert a candle.

Ask your grocer for Belgium lettuce or mushroom baskets. Arrange fruits and vegetables or small potted plants in one for a centerpiece, or line it with colorful cloth to make a breadbasket.

Keep an airtight container of chocolate curls in your freezer to make a dessert look exquisite. Melt chocolate in a double boiler and spread a thin layer on the back of a cookie sheet. Refrigerate until firm, then use a metal spatula to scrape the chocolate from the cookie sheet, forming curls.

Have quick-burning logs on hand for an instant fire in the fireplace.

Buy extra pomegranates and artichokes in season and let them dry out. Sprinkle with potpourri oil and display them in a pretty bowl.

Fix and freeze your favorite company casserole. Label with oven temperature and baking time. Use it when you have unexpected company.

Copy your dinner-party recipes on index cards. Tie them up with ribbon and give to your guests when they leave.

Turn ordinary lemonade into fruit punch by mixing it with an equal amount of grape juice.

When you're planning a buffet,
choose foods for your menu that
will look fresh after sitting out
for an extended period of time.

"An opportunity grasped and used produces at least one other opportunity." —Chester A. Swor

The first time you treat your family to a spur-of-the-moment celebration, they'll probably be surprised. One of them is likely to suggest another.

Serve lemonade in sixteen-ounce canning jars at a casual party. Garnish each jar with a citrus fruit slice and colorful drinking straw.

Create beautiful cloth napkins and tablecloths from cotton chintz fabric. For napkins, cut twenty-two-inch squares of fabric. For a tablecloth, cut the fabric ten inches longer and wider than the table. Hem by machine or with stitchless glue.

Sprinkle popcorn with seasoned salt, taco seasoning, or Parmesan cheese for a different snack.

If you want to invite more people than you can seat for dinner, make an extra table for six. Use a jigsaw to cut a four-foot circle from interior plywood. Sand the edges. Place it on top of a card table and cover it with a round tablecloth that extends to the floor.

For a last-minute dessert, melt eight ounces of chocolate in a double boiler, stirring occasionally until smooth. Add one-half teaspoon of peppermint extract. Pour into a heat-proof serving bowl and surround with round, butter-flavored crackers for dipping.

Create a holiday tree to use all year long. Place a two-foot manzanita branch (available at craft stores) into a one-pound coffee can and fill the can with plaster of paris, anchoring the branch in place. Hide the can by bunching up colorful fabric and tying it around the top of the can with pretty ribbon. Hang miniature seasonal ornaments from the branches.

Make an easy but elegant centerpiece. Carve the centers from three red cabbages. Use them to hold fresh flowers.

At an appropriate time, give a toast to the guests who have chosen to be with you at a special occasion.

"Begin the day with friendliness and only friends you'll find."
—Frank B. Whitney

When you have a party, fix a plate of goodies and take it to a homebound friend.

Use a fabric-covered journal to create a memory scrapbook of a party. Ask guests to sign their names and write a message. Put pictures from the party in the book.

Bake a sheet cake. Carve the first initial of the guest of honor and frost the initial. Place it on a pretty platter and surround it with ivy.

Nestle a large bowl inside a larger basket. Fill in the gap between the containers with parsley and fresh flowers. Use it to serve a salad.

Rent a tank of helium and blow up dozens of balloons. Use one-yard lengths of curling ribbon and tie one balloon to the back of each chair. Place them in bunches around the perimeter of the room or cover your entrance hall ceiling with balloons letting the curling ribbons hang down.

Help your daughter make a keepsake of the first flowers she receives. When the flowers wither, save the dried petals to make potpourri with a few drops of fragrance oil. Put them in a pretty bowl in her room.

Serve carbonated grape juice in wine glasses to toast a family member's accomplishment—making a sports team, landing a new job, passing a test.

Dip apples, pears, and bunches of grapes in egg whites, then roll them in sugar. Let dry, then mound in a big glass bowl for a beautiful decoration.

Lower the temperature in your home before a party.

Make a tablecloth liner by cutting a flannel blanket or sheet the size of the table plus several inches overhang. This will give an elegant, slightly padded effect to your tablecloth.

To give your home a cozy aroma, simmer a few whole cloves, a sliced apple, and some orange peeling in enough water to cover.

Plan to have a birthday cake delivered to your office the first day of every month. Celebrate the birthdays of anyone who was born that month.

When choosing fresh flowers for an occasion, remember that irises wilt quickly. Choose heartier flowers such as daisies, lilies, carnations, or astromelia.

Ask interior designers and furniture stores for their out-of-date fabric samples to make napkins, table runners, basket liners, and small pillows.

"Let us always meet each other with a smile, for the smile is the beginning of love."

—Mother Teresa

No matter whether you're having a family dinner or a large party, greet everyone who comes in your door with a smile.

Before a party, line several paper grocery sacks with plastic garbage bags and hide them in your laundry room or pantry. The bags will stand up for easier cleaning up after the party.

On your child's birthday, include several treats in her lunch to share with friends on this special day.

Make a fabulous fruit and flower stacked center-piece. You'll need three graduated-size plates and two champagne glasses. Tier the plates, starting with the largest on the bottom, placing a glass in between the plates. Arrange fruit on top of each plate. Fill in gaps with greenery. Place cut flowers into stem vials and tuck into the greenery.

Save the newspapers from important dates—the births of your children, marriage days, and graduation days. Mount them in frames.

Chill salad plates in your freezer for twenty minutes before dinner.

Use decorative tassels as napkin rings for a dressy dinner party.

Throw a pasta party. Make simple tablecloths from red-and-white-checked fabric. Tie raffia or bandannas around the necks of old wine bottles and use them as vases or candleholders. Arrange baguettes and fresh flowers in an ordinary basket for a centerpiece.

Help your kids make and hang paper-doll style garlands to decorate for a celebration.

Send guests home from your house with a small remembrance of the occasion. Wrap cookies in cellophane and tie with a bow; share a small jar of homemade sauce or jam; give parsley, planted in a small clay pot, for snipping.

Hide small presents and treats and have a family treasure hunt on Valentine's Day.

Take photos at a special celebration. Write the date and event on the back of each picture and send copies to each guest who attended.

"People need joy quite as much as clothing. Some of them need it far more." —Margaret Colier Graham

Notice and mark occasions of joy with small, impromptu gatherings of family or friends.

Decorate plain cupcakes with colored coconut. Put some coconut in a self-closing plastic bag. Add several drops of food coloring and shake the bag until the coconut is the color you want.

Have a sack of cookies ready to give your college student for the drive back to school.

Make your own fruit baskets to give to friends. Ask your grocer for Belgium endive boxes. Fill them with fruit and nuts. Wrap with cellophane and tie with a pretty bow.

Bring spring flowers into your home early by forcing blooms from shrubs. When buds begin to swell on flowering shrubs, cut off a few branches and put them in a vase of water.

Line serving platters with non-toxic leaves, such as fig, ivy, or galax leaves. Use for serving sliced cheese, crackers, and fruit.

For a special-occasion drink, serve non-alcoholic daiquiris or margaritas out of festive glasses.

Make herbed vinegar for party favors. Put a clove of garlic and several sprigs of rosemary, tarragon, or basil into a sterilized bottle. Heat cider vinegar to 160 degrees, then pour it over the herbs. Tightly close up the container with a cork or lid. Let it sit for two weeks to bring out the flavor of the herbs.

For a quick, yet fancy salad, hollow out a tomato. Fill it with one artichoke heart, then place it on a lettuce leaf. Cover it with bleu-cheese dressing.

Keep your camera ready with film and fresh batteries so you can capture special occasions.

Save a length of this year's Christmas tree trunk to burn as next year's "Yule Log."

Let your children decorate cookies for their class-mates on a special day. Buy tubes of icing with decorating tips and decorate sugar cookies.

Before houseguests arrive, sprinkle a little perfumed powder over clean bedsheets to give them a wonderful fragrance.

Add excitement to a plain chocolate cake mix by adding two teaspoons of peppermint flavoring to the ingredients called for on the box. Frost with chocolate frosting and sprinkle crushed peppermint candies on the top.

Keep a stuffed bear dressed for the season and on display in your home.

Warm up a winter evening with hot almond milk. Stir almond flavoring and sugar, to taste, into heated milk. Serve in mugs.

Serve hamburgers on Lincoln's birthday and call them Gettysburgers.

"A happy family is but an earlier heaven."
—Sir John Browning

Make a list of things that make your family happy. Read it often.

Keep little paper umbrellas on hand and use them in drinks to add a little fun to a meal.

Get into the habit of playing soft classical music at dinnertime, and eat by candlelight often. Let your family know they are just as important as company.

Add a few drops of green food coloring to eggs before you scramble them. Surprise your kids with a "Green Eggs and Ham" breakfast.

Make Easter baskets with real grass. Fill plastic basket liners with soil and plant fescue seeds. Keep moist and watch the grass grow. Put candy eggs and other treats in the grass on Easter day.

When your college daughter comes home for a visit, put fresh flowers in her room to show you were anticipating her visit.

Tie big bows on your sofa pillows at Christmas to make them look like presents.

"Cleaning your house while your kids are still growing is like shoveling the walk before it stops snowing."
—Phyllis Diller

Today, instead of cleaning your house, do something fun with your child.

Cut the top off of a pumpkin and clean out the inside. Use it as a soup tureen during autumn.

For quick and different cookies, roll out a package of prepared pie crusts. Cut out shapes with cookie cutters. Sprinkle with cinnamon and sugar, and bake on a cookie sheet for eight minutes at 350 degrees.

For family reunion favors, use paint pens to personalize sun visors or plastic glasses.

Send funny cards to friends or family members on April Fool's Day. Sign them from a mystery friend.

Create a scarecrow for your yard. Dress it in different outfits, according to the season of the year.

When your child wins a contest or is elected to a school office, fill several large plastic garbage bags with balloons. Ask him to sit in a chair with his eyes closed. Stand on a ladder behind him and pour the balloons on top of him. Take a picture!

Order napkins monogrammed with your family's name. Use them to dress up an event.

"When someone does something good, applaud! You will make two people happy."   —Samuel Golden

Make or find a recording of a cheering crowd. Play it as a family member who's done something neat walks in the door.

Make a delicious punch by using club soda in place of water when mixing frozen fruit-juice concentrate.

Turn an ordinary cake into a clever landscape Frost the cake, mounding extra icing to make hills. Use green-tinted coconut to make grass, and sprinkle crushed chocolate cookies to make dirt. Create a scene with small plastic toys and animals.

Serve all red foods for dinner on Valentine's Day, orange and black foods on Halloween, and green foods on St. Patrick's Day.

Create an autumn porch light. Carve stars all over a large pumpkin. Place a candle inside.

"Offer hospitality to one another."

—I Peter 4:9

Host a "New Kid on the Block" party for a new neighbor. Make it potluck, and have old neighbors exchange names and phone numbers with the newcomers.

For a change at dinner, use a colorful quilt as a tablecloth.

At Christmastime, set white votive candles in a clear glass bowl of coarse salt to make a "candles in the snow" centerpiece.

When friends drop in unexpectedly on a cold day, fix a warm chocolate mint drink. Pour hot cocoa over a peppermint tea bag. Steep to taste.

Fill a child's closet with balloons for a surprise.

Take a small gift to your host or hostess.

When a family member or friend can't be with you to celebrate an occasion, have everyone present hold up a big sign that says "We miss you!" Take a picture and mail it to the missing person.

Create a romantic atmosphere one night by using only candlelight in your home.

At your Thanksgiving feast, have everyone around the table take turns saying what they are most thankful for.

Make an ice-cream pie. Firmly press slightly softened ice-cream into a graham cracker crust. Spread fudge topping over the top and sprinkle with chopped nuts. Freeze until ready to serve.

Roast pumpkin seeds on an autumn day. Scoop seeds out of a pumpkin and rinse them. Place them on a cookie sheet, sprinkle with salt, and bake at 350 degrees for ten minutes or until brown and crunchy.

Start a collection for each of your children. Add to it at Christmas and on birthdays.

"A little nonsense now and then, is relished by the wisest men."   —Anonymous
Designate a family dinner "joke night."

Dress up your dog or cat for a special event with a big plaid ribbon around its neck.

Make a big deal out of someone's graduation. Take a photo of the graduate to a film-processing store and have a poster made.

Keep tiny American flags on hand to decorate foods on patriotic holidays.

When you add small embellishments to the ordinary details of life, you turn these things into activities that celebrate being alive. Take a batch of freshly baked cookies and a thermos of cold milk for the kids in your carpool.

Burn Pinon incense in your fireplace to add pizazz to a cold winter night.

Make a princess cake for a young girl. Bake a bundt cake according to directions. Unmold it, then place a ten- to twelve-inch doll in the center hole. Frost the cake to look like the doll's formal gown.

Garnish a cup of clear broth with a sprig of parsley.

Serve fresh blueberries or raspberries in stemmed glasses for an easy but elegant dessert.

On a cold afternoon, bake chocolate-chip cookies and have them cooling on cookie racks when your children get home from school.

Provide finger bowls after eating finger foods. Float a rose petal in a small bowl of warm, lemon-flavored water.

Wrap a package in grosgrain ribbon or satin fabric scraps to make it elegant.

Make an ice-cream cake. Line two, eight-inch cake pans with plastic wrap and pack your favorite ice cream into each pan. Smooth the tops and freeze. Unmold, then quickly fill and frost the layers. Return it to the freezer until firm.

Help your kids make gift baskets for Dad on Father's Day. Line a basket with a bandanna and fill it with items you know he'd like—fishing paraphernalia, small tools, photo supplies.

Host a mother-daughter luncheon on Mother's Day for your daughter, her friends, and their mothers.

Keep a costume box in a closet for impromptu skits and events.

Dip the rim of iced tea glasses
first in lemon juice, then in sugar
for a special effect.

Be ready to make a fresh flower arrangement for any occasion. Keep a collection of vases, pruning shears, blocks of oasis, arranging frogs, and dried baby's breath on hand.

Write the birthdays of family members and friends on your calendar so you won't forget to do something to make their day special.

"Every home where love abides and friendship is a guest, is surely home, and home, sweet home for there the heart can rest." —Henry Van Dyke

Designate a "rest" night. Fix an easy dinner, unplug the phone, curl up in quilts, and enjoy an old movie together.

Have a tea party for your daughter and several of her friends.

Celebrate your child's first haircut. Take pictures and save some hair clippings in a small envelope.

Deliver helium balloons to someone's workplace on an important day.

"Let us go singing as far as we go; the road will be less tedious."   —Virgil
When your family or friends are going through tough times, it's the best time to celebrate any and every day.

On a winter day, celebrate the fun you had as a family on last summer's vacation. Get out pictures and reminisce. Talk about where you want to go next summer.

Have a family awards night. Give personalized awards for silly categories such as fastest dish washer, best lawn mower, and quickest to answer the phone.

Start a tradition of going out to eat at your college student's favorite hometown restaurant the night before he travels back to school.

Freeze orange juice in ice trays
to use in orange juice
so it won't get watery.

"They will celebrate your abundant goodness and joyfully sing of your righteousness."   —Psalm 145:7

Have a seasonal party to celebrate God's abundance. Serve fruits and vegetables in season.

For an easy hors d'ouevres, boil small red potatoes and serve with various dips—guacamole, ranch, or onion.

Fold one-half cup of crushed peppermint candies into a chocolate or white cake mix and bake as directed.

When a friend has a new baby, make a door decoration by attaching various small baby toys and a huge pink or blue bow to a grapevine wreath.

Make the most of a few fresh flowers. Fill a vase with sprays of ivy and tall, thin green branches, and arrange the flowers against the background. Attach a note of congratulations and place it on a coworker's desk.

Give events added meaning by keeping a special occasion scrapbook. Include pictures of recitals and parties, signatures of teachers and friends who attended, and souvenirs such as ticket stubs and programs.

Send Mother's Day or Father's Day cards to your sister, brother, former college roommates, and other close friends.

Let your child decorate her bedroom door for various holidays.

Celebrate someone's half-birthday—usually an uneventful day—with half of a birthday cake.

Make a big deal out of your child's first paycheck. Have an enlarged copy made of it, and put it in a frame.

Get out the nice serving pieces you usually save for company and use them for your family.

Send your mother flowers on your birthday to thank her for bringing you into the world.

Host a come-as-you-are party for your child's friends. Get up early and drive to the guests' homes to pick them up—as they are. Go back to your house for a great breakfast.

Hold hands when you say grace at the table.

Send a family photo with your Christmas card each year. Your friends will appreciate it.

"Special occasions are the exclamation points of life."
—Anonymous

Celebrate the usual events, and invent unusual ones to celebrate as well.

Spray cologne on a letter before sending it to someone you care for.

Collect pretty aprons and wear one when cooking or cleaning house. If you don't enjoy these tasks, a pretty apron can help.

"It is possible to give away and become richer."
—Proverbs 11:24

As a family, give your time to the less fortunate. Serve food at a homeless shelter or visit a nursing home.

Mail a college student inexpensive door or room decorations for different holidays and seasons.

During the week of your children's birthdays, allow them to arrange and display their collections in the family room.

When citrus fruits are in season, make breakfast extra special by squeezing fresh juice.

Keep a party journal. Record the date, time, location, guestlist, menu, decorations, and costs. After the party, make notes of what you did right and mistakes you want to avoid next time. This will be valuable information when planning your next party.

Decorate the room of a hospitalized family member or friend with balloons, crepe paper and inspirational posters. Create a giant get-well card from poster board. Take it to the patient's office or school for friends to sign.

Make a Yule Log cake. Bake a cake mix in two one-pound coffee cans. Lay the cakes end to end, and frost with chocolate icing. Use the tines of a fork to make bark-like marks on the "log." Decorate with candies.

Spray magnolia leaves with gold paint to use as place cards. Print guests' names on the leaves with a felt-tipped black calligraphy pen.

Make chocolate cups for a beautiful dessert. Slowly melt chocolate in a double boiler. Use a pastry brush to paint melted chocolate on the insides of paper cupcake cups. Let dry and peel off the paper. Use the chocolate cups to hold ice cream, mousse, or pudding.

Order red- or green-tinted bread from your bakery to serve during the Christmas holidays.

Create inexpensive tables for parties by purchasing damaged wooden doors and placing them on top of wooden horses. Cover with floor-length tablecloths.

In autumn, put a brightly colored chrysanthemum plant in a carved out pumpkin beside your front door.

Make your ceiling shimmer for a party. Cut out dozens of silver stars in various sizes and hang them from your ceiling with fishing line and straight pins.

Just before company comes, put some potpourri oil on a cotton ball and vacuum it into your sweeper. Vacuum around your house and leave a pleasant fragrance in the air.

Dress up and be your own singing telegram to a family member or friend.

"If you make children happy now, you will make them happy twenty years hence by the memory of it."

—Kate Douglas Wiggan

Use toothpicks to roast miniature marshmallows over candlelight with a child.

Give a retiree a "Gone Fishin'" knapsack. Place small fishing paraphernalia, candies, and gum in the center of a large bandanna. Tie up the four corners and attach it to a cane pole.

When your family gathers for the holidays, videotape the oldest living relative reading the Christmas story. Continue this tradition through the years and build a treasury of memories of grandparents, aunts, and uncles.

Make an ice-cream watermelon for a summer get-together. Line a bowl with lime sherbet, one inch thick. Freeze hard. Stir a handful of miniature chocolate-chip "seeds" into raspberry sherbet and fill in the center on top of the lime sherbet. Refreeze. To serve, unmold on a plate and slice the "watermelon."

"I value this delicious home feeling as one of the choicest gifts a parent can bestow." —Washington Irving Have an "at home" party for just your family.

Shop at antique stores for old magazines issued on the birth months and years of friends. Give them as birthday gifts.

On Valentine's Day tint your children's hot cereal pink and sprinkle with red hots.

Use sparklers to decorate birthday cakes.

At Christmastime, put a small tree in your kitchen and decorate it with cooking and food items such as cookie cutters, wooden spoons, and garlands of popcorn.

Throw a backwards party. Write the invitations backwards so they can only be read by holding them up to a mirror, ask guests to wear their clothes backwards, and start the meal with dessert. This is especially fun for a child's birthday party.

Have a "Grandma Shower" for a friend who's going to be a grandmother.

Paint names on dyed Easter eggs to use as place cards for a spring luncheon.

Blow up several balloons and attach them to your mailbox when you're expecting out-of-town guests.

Use clear fishing line to string dried apple and orange slices, cinnamon sticks and bay leaves to make holiday garlands.

Stud small apples with whole cloves
and float in a bowl of hot cider.
Serve with gingersnap cookies
at a fall open house.

Make wrapping paper to match each occasion. Wrap the gift in white paper and draw appropriate designs with paint pens.

Create a giant gingerbread bear for a children's party. Combine one gingerbread mix with one-third cup of water. Form the dough into a large gingerbread bear and bake in a preheated oven at 350 degrees for twenty-five minutes or until lightly brown.

"When friends meet, hearts warm."   —John Ray
Have an appreciation luncheon with close friends. The purpose is to tell each other what you like about each other.

Give a "Rice Bag" luncheon for a bride to be. Invite close friends of the bride, and after lunch let everyone help make little rice bags for the wedding.

Tie up vintage cotton kitchen towels with raffia for napkins at a casual dinner party.

Hang Christmas garlands from the backs of dining-room chairs.

Plan a tailgate party before a football game. Get corsage boxes from a florist. Line the inside with a colorful napkin. Place the food inside, then tie up the box with team-color ribbons.

Collect pretty fall leaves. Press them in a book for a few days, then use them to form a runner down the center of your dining table. Place an arrangement of fall vegetables and candles in the middle.

To make paper napkins more elegant, fold two contrasting colored napkins together. Tie them up with a ribbon and ruffle out the tops to show the colors.

Slowly melt a package of caramels. Serve with apple slices for dipping.

Make beautiful, yet inexpensive, candlesticks for a special occasion. Buy old candlesticks made of metal or glass at a flea market. Paint the candlesticks with gold-leaf paint.

Take popcorn pumpkins to the office on Halloween. Make or buy popcorn balls. Wrap them up in squares of orange crepe paper, gathering the paper at the top to form a pumpkin shape. Tie on green curly ribbon or raffia to make the stems.

If you're using rented equipment for a special occasion, have the items delivered as early as possible. Check off each item and make sure it works before the driver leaves.

Make a giant cookie greeting. Spread prepared refrigerated cookie dough into a fifteen-inch circle and bake. Decorate and write a message on the top using tubes of icing.

Create a quick but elegant centerpiece by grouping several votive candles on a twelve-inch square of mirror. (Mirror squares are available at hardware stores.)

"It seems to me I spent my life in carpools. But you know, that's how I kept track with what was going on."
—Barbara Bush

Buy a good singalong tape to enjoy with your kids in the car.

Call your local high school to inquire about band students who play in string quartets or combos. This is usually an inexpensive way to have live music for an occasion.

If you don't have a fireplace, hang Christmas stockings from the backs of your dining-room chairs.

Buy vintage saucers, plates, or bowls at flea markets and use them to hold cookies, baked bread, or a cheeseball for gifts.

Give personalized party favors at a summer party. Plant small marigolds in four-inch terra-cotta pots. Tie a bow around the top of the pot. Use paint pens to write guests' names on the side of the pot.

Create a pretty table covering. First, cover the table with a length of colored fabric. Then put a layer of nylon netting or inexpensive lace over the colored cloth. Tie up the corners with pretty ribbons.

For a teenager's party, make a three- to five-foot submarine sandwich. Line up foot-long sandwich buns on a long piece of foil-covered cardboard. Layer favorite sub-sandwich toppings and cut the sandwiches into serving pieces so it looks like one long sandwich.

Serve black-eyed peas on New Year's Day, the old-time tradition of wishing good fortune for the new year.

Buy a length of netting or inexpensive lace and dip it in brewed tea. Let it dry, iron it, and use as an "antique" lace tablecloth.

Order pink-tinted bread from your bakery for Valentine's Day. Cut out hearts with a cookie cutter to make Valentine sandwiches.

Host an around-the-clock wedding shower. Assign each guest to a different hour of the day and ask them to bring a gift that the newlyweds can use during that time of day.

Make round bread for special sandwiches by baking bread mixes in coffee cans.

Fix chocolate apples for dessert. Push a wooden skewer into the end of each apple. Use a pastry brush to paint melted chocolate on the apples until completely coated. Set them on waxed paper to dry. If you like, sprinkle the apples with nuts while they're still wet.

Dress up your windows for a special occasion. Use greenery garlands, fresh or silk, to tie back curtains or drapes.

Line the walkway to your door with white twinkle lights for a party.

If you need to wrap a pretty package and all you have is creased ribbon, run the ribbon through a curling iron to straighten it.

When taking photographs at a special occasion, wrap toilet paper or tissue around the flash to create a picture with a softer effect.

Organize a neighborhood yard-decorating contest at Christmas. Appoint a committee of judges. The winner receives a plate of goodies from the losers.

Send a college student a final-exams survival kit. Include a mug and instant cocoa mix, energy bars, pens and pencils, highlighter markers, and sticky-back notes.

Add your own flair to packaged
refrigerated cookie dough.
Stir in nuts, butterscotch morsels,
or chopped dried apricots
and bake as directed.

Make take-out food look elegant by garnishing with carrot curls, sprigs of herbs, or lettuce leaves.

Don't worry if you're having more people over than you have matching china. Mix up different patterns. The effect is charming.

Always keep an extra bag of ice in your freezer.

To get a dinner table conversation started, ask each guest to tell where they were when a significant event occurred. For example, ask "Where were you when President Kennedy was shot?" or "Where were you when the first men landed on the moon?"

Create an easy centerpiece. Spray fruits and vegetables with nonstick cooking oil. Polish them with a paper towel and arrange in a big bowl or on a platter. Snip sprigs from green shrubs to fill in holes.

Celebrate the first fire in the fireplace this winter.
Fix popcorn and hot cocoa and sit by the fire with
someone you love.

Save the flowers from your daughter's wedding.
Let them dry out, then make a wreath for her new home
with the dried flowers.

To celebrate a special day in someone's life, send a letter and a self-addressed stamped envelope to friends of the honoree, asking them to write a warm greeting and send it back to you secretly. Collect the messages and present them to the honoree.

Give someone a gift of personal coupons. Instead of buying a present, write down different "gifts" she can redeem.

Help your children celebrate the end of each grading period with their favorite dessert.

When a young child is learning a certain color or letter of the alphabet, plan a dinner menu with foods of that color or that begin with that letter.

Make a cookie bouquet. Decorate sugar cookies to look like flowers. Use Royal Icing to "glue" the cookies to the tops of wooden skewers. Stick the skewers into a flower pot filled with a piece of Styrofoam, forming an arrangement. Cover the Styrofoam with green jelly beans. (Royal Icing: Beat together two cups of powdered sugar and one egg white. Add a little water if it's too stiff.)

Run ribbons or streamers down the length of your dining table for a quick, festive touch.

Make a plain tablecloth festive by drawing simple designs with paint pens.

On New Year's Day decide on a family motto for the year, like "Life's too short not to celebrate," or "Everyday's a gift."

For a backyard party, serve iced-down drinks from a #3 galvanized tub.

At a birthday dinner, ask each person to say something that's wonderful and unique about the celebrant.

Celebrate your son getting his braces off. Give him a basket of previously off-limit treats like candy and gum, a new toothbrush, and some dental floss. Serve foods for dinner he hasn't been able to eat for a while.

Buy a Santa hat for Mom or Dad to wear when handing out presents Christmas morning.

Host a mother-of-the-bride survival party for a friend whose child is getting married. Have guests bring fun gifts like aspirin and antacids, as well as nice gifts like picture frames and pretty handkerchiefs.

Ask each dinner-party guest to bring a fresh flower. Arrange the flowers in a vase. Take a picture of the group and the arrangement. Print the date, occasion, and a warm message on the back of the pictures and mail copies to guests as a memento of the evening.

Tie big raffia bows around seasonal fruits and vegetables for instant decorations—melons in summer, pumpkins in fall, gourds in winter.

Decorate your child's bedroom on a special day with streamers, balloons, and small hidden presents.

"He who laughs, lasts!"　　　—Mary Pettibone Poole
Plan a small gathering of friends. Ask everyone to bring a joke or funny story to share.

For a quick centerpiece, arrange three chubby candles on a flat dish and cover the surface with sphagnum moss. Arrange baby's breath, greenery, and a few flowers on the moss.

To host a child's birthday or other party, dress up as his or her favorite character.

Learn a couple of fancy napkin folds, or make up your own.

Celebrate New Year's Eve with children by saving candle stubs all year long. Cover a table with brown paper. Just before midnight, light them all. Then at midnight, blow them out and everybody makes wishes for the year.

Make a welcome-home banner for a college student who's returning home.

Keep a guestbook for your friends to sign when they come to your home.

Keep unfilled cream puffs in the freezer. They can be filled with chicken or tuna salad for a quick lunch or with ice cream for an instant dessert.

Buy a pastry bag and practice your own cake decorating designs on the back of a cookie sheet. Scrape off the frosting and put it back in the bag for more practice.

Create a chocolate-sculpture centerpiece for an event. Buy a papier-mâché animal at a craft store. (A swan, bear, or rabbit works well.) Use a pastry brush to paint several coats of melted chocolate onto the animal, giving it a solid chocolate appearance. Let dry, then set on a platter and surround with greenery.

Give your child sixteen shares of stock on his or her sixteenth birthday.

Have a "You're My Hero" party for your husband or son. Make a list of all the things you love about him. Fix his favorite dinner.

When you're setting up a buffet, pull the table away from the walls so there's plenty of room to circulate around it.

When you're having dinner guests, try not to serve anything that has to be cooked or fussed over at the last minute.

Help elderly neighbors decorate their home for special occasions.

Begin a collection of holiday china to use in December.

Give your son or daughter an old-fashioned hope chest for his or her thirteenth birthday. Begin to stock it with items they will need when they leave home—cookware, tools, linens—items pertaining to their special interests.

Let your children make yogurt popsicles on a hot summer day. Mix two cups of yogurt with a six-ounce can of frozen orange juice and pour it into small paper cups. Insert a popsicle stick into each one and freeze. Peel away the paper and enjoy.

Give a potted geranium to a friend who is moving away. The geranium stands for remembrance.

Give your dinner table an elegant feel by placing one votive candle at each place setting.

Help your child celebrate your family pet's birthday or adoption day. Give the pet a bath, brushing, and a new toy.

Send a celebration kit to your college student with instructions to open after final exams are over. Include confetti, balloons, and treats.

Organize a neighborhood Fourth of July parade on your street. Decorate bicycles, wagons, and other riding toys with streamers and balloons. End up at your house for watermelon.

Keep your dining-room table set with pretty place mats and dishes for your family. You'll all look forward to dinner together.

Bake a heart-shaped cake and give it to friends on their wedding anniversary.

Make a fancy box for collecting Valentines or other letters. Cover a square box and lid with Victorian print wrapping paper. Glue paper doilies on each side, and tie up the box with gold cord.

Search at flea markets for a vintage crocheted bedspread to use as a tablecloth.

Make your own gourmet cinnamon coffee. For eight cups, add one-half teaspoon of cinnamon to grounds.

About the author:

Judie Byrd has spent a lifetime learning to inject those "little extras" into life and finds great joy in sharing her ideas with others through her seminars, books, and videos. She has attended cooking classes around the world, including Cordon Bleu in London. But in her seminars and publications she stresses that creating special times for family and friends doesn't require a lot of time, money, or training. Judie and her husband recently opened their second family-run restaurant and are planning to franchise the operation. Judie is co-author of *A Mother's Manual for Holiday Survival* and co-producer of the *Holiday Survival* video series and has also written for *Family Circle* magazine. She has been married twenty-eight years and has three grown children.